The Gospel According

. . . to Mary

poems by

Carl Winderl

Finishing Line Press
Georgetown, Kentucky

The Gospel According

. . . to Mary

Publisher: Leah Huete de Maines

Editor: Christen Kincaid

Cover Art: *Virgin Annuciate,* by Antonello da Messina (1430—1479), Italian
        Renaissance painter. As the story goes, Mary the Mother of Jesus
        was alone with the scriptures in her prayer closet when the angel
        Gabriel appeared to her with his Announcement.
        Creative Commons CC0

Author Photo: Marcus Emerson, MarcusEmerson@pointloma.edu

Cover Design: Elizabeth Maines McCleavy

Order online: www.finishinglinepress.com
        also available on amazon.com

Author inquiries and mail orders:
Finishing Line Press
P. O. Box 1626
Georgetown, Kentucky 40324
U. S. A.

Table of Contents

for my grandmothers
Marie Myslenski, née Trojanski
and
Bernice Bertha Brooks, née Davis

who would be pleased

an immaculate conception

in the basement of the broadview
of all places
i go to sit and do my laundry

and to commune with my soul

the washers whirl and swish
the soiled clothes
while i sit
sensing the cleansing

rinsing to a frenetic spinstop
they tumble to
an arid staleness

finally
morosely, I await to wear
the soilless linen in an unclean world

the Gospel According

. . . to Mary

Agni Dei

Isaac without spot or blemish
about to be slain lay
there
before Him

trussed up, in trust

his father's arm poised
the death angel
hovering near, thoughts

racing, fear of

the known, and the unknown;
but neither squirm, nor blanch
did I see
in Him pinioned there, nary

a tremor on His lips

while He looked upon
His *stabat mater . . .*

as
to me He whispered His
Job-like words

: though He may kill Me
  yet will I

  trust Him

in Pilate's wash water

floated My Son's sins

: innocence, obedience
  allegiance
  and long sufferance

while the chief priests, scribes
and elders
circled round, in a frenzy
smelling

blood in the water, although
'twas theirs

not His, and yet

not all alone Whose mother
stood outside the praetorium gate
and heard

from he who sitteth in the seat of
Gabbatha, "see ye to it"

the flagellated snap of
the CX whiplashes on Him
bound to the pillar

Who used to succor at my breast

yielded He
His back to be beaten,
His beard to be plucked,
His Mother to seek help from He

Who dispels disgrace

whilst His flinty face shielded He
not from buffets nor from the spitting
so that His blood
be upon them and upon

their children
witnessed, a scourged Jesus (Who

   suffered them, to
   come unto Him) and whose
parents' bloody deeds
live

long ever after

Theotokos

I'm "The Mother of God"
ever
at the foot of the Cross clutching at

Simeon's sword impaled in my breast

where the blood of despair trickles
betwixt my fingers
as the sword pierces next

my heart, my mind, my
soul, my very being there
washes me
in the blood of the
Lamb, again, as at His birth

while the rabble twist and turn the

blade with their jeers and scorn, and
their catcalls taunting Him to

save Himself, let alone the world

til only me, I'm left with just
His striped God-forsaken Body. I
sink to my knees, praying
my prayer to doubt
my doubt that true to His Word

He will

do what He said He would do,
three days hence; and my wounds

will be no more. Forever.

on Good Friday afternoon

on Good Friday afternoon, or there-
about when they stretched

My Son to cool

the heavens clouded o'er with
opaque, lethal smoke chok-
ing the eye of the sun
from the Ffathers above, and below

though the leaded sky was
not a nebulous phenomenon but
a simple chemical reaction

$: (HCN + [CO_2 + O_2 + N] + \alpha) 6 \times 10^6 @ K^\circ F$

yielding a noxious gray holocaust sky

and the rains that came that eve
in single carbon droplets fell
from the eyes of souls winging above

not from despair but joy

for the long-expected Messiah had come
and gone

to prepare a place for them

while My Son hung there

on His tree
I pondered in my heart

not just that Tree in the Garden but

the other trees there in Gethsemane
and where were the mothers
of those two others

flanking Him, and were their

criminal hearts black as coal
with sin and hung there for no-good
evil as they say
today, whom He came to save, . . .

was one heart anthracite and
the other bitumen—and were they

diamonds in the rough, for

certain My Son knows
the secret of compressing a heart
so dark into pure carats, but

I wonder,
which is easier

: anthracite or bitumen

or if . . . it is easy
hanging there, on His Cross . . . all
for a creature of the dust
of the ground, or for

a lump of coal

I see My Son, still

up on the Cross
His face ashen, and

adorned in the fashionable pin-
stripes of Dachau, Belsen, Bremen,
and Auschwitz, *et al.:* yes, all
in gray and white
and on His breast emblazoned

: the yellow star of David

(for Him a family crest) but for
all else a
monogram, of sorts; and wound about
His Head a crown
of triple barbed wire, and
on each wrist, nailed
arm's width apart for all to see

: a linear Numerican blue tattoo

so that when they take
Him down
they'll forever know

He's the One

to put into their ovens, ignite
the gas, turn up
to 6 million°F, and cook
Him too, and
when He's done

they take His body out, break it,
and serve Him
to me

. . . and you

what did they expect

when they pricked My Son

on the Cross
circling in, like so many
furies, harpies, (about
   to abscise the Rose

   of Sharon from

   the Tree of Jesse) and the
eumenides

as if their own trinitarian tribe

of a kind as
manunkind whom I pity

not because of their busy-
ness but because
their learnedness misread the

signs & cosines from the axis above

especially from Isaiah, who hath
prophesied, born of a virgin

shall ye know
the Word was made flesh
at my breast
with eyes, hands, organs, and

passions
to heal, to tickle, to die
: afterall,

   doth not a Jew bleed?

Amor omnia vincit

to transfirgure the Trinity
first
the three-dimensional physical
must be entered

and conquered

or else *Amor omnia vincit* proves false
for

at what depth
must the cross brace be buried
to sustain
the weight of the Cross above
My Son hung upon

of how much girth
should those timbers
have been adzed
to support the burden of
sin
they nailed to that Cross

and

from what height
did those sweatdrops of blood
descend to cleanse
the dirty hands, filthy hearts,
and bestial souls
of those

sullied crucifiers
He set free

when He breathed
at last
consummatum est, for whom

so that from my own corner
of omniscience,
sunt rerum lacrimae's the price

thus I now see and I know
it's not just a hypothesis, nor
a theory

it is Law

at Judas' funeral

by his mother I
stood un-

alone, as Mother of
mothers, while the others draped
in black, gaped at

My Monday mourning blue,
in grief united

as are our boys
eternally,
on this so fair and foul a morn
whence in uni-
Son once
below,
and

on earth

him now lies
that He might rise

as It is in heaven

so that at his grave
where our mothers' tears (Mine
  slid down my
  other cheek) water
the dirt,

near his mother's feet (among
  women) I lay

anon a sad bouquet, so ophelian

of pansies, poppies, daisies
and of

oh, our sweet babies' breath

after His death

when I first read
in His memoirs
"the Word became Flesh"

I thought of His tattoos

and the time I first
discovered them:

as I cleansed His body
with the soothing oils
and preserving ointments—

(in preparation for His
   Ultimate Rebirth)

the first
on His right bicep
in Blue Old English, outlined
in Black and quotated,
"Born to Raze Hell!"

the second, inside His left forearm
vibrant in Green & Red
depicted a writhing, hissing Serpent
impaled upon a stake

and the third, over His breast
a pink Valentine's Heart
with jagged, red edges
broken in two

on one half, the Black
bold Capitals M-O-T
and, on the other, H-E-R

so that
there
even there, at the last
I saw
as I tore the white linen
into strips still
again to wrap His Body

He was
Mystery and Discovery, just as

in the beginning . . .
. . . until
it was finished. (Or was it. I
   wonder if

   He was, . . .) Yes,
and always is
and ever will be

Mystery and Discovery
for me: the Enigma

unto Revelation

Why in April . . .

they impaled My very Heart
on a wooden stake
planted on the skull of a hill; My

flesh they stretched arms-
length to dry
flayed upon a Nazi kite (its
  Cross spar silhouettes
  the twilight Friday sky) a
totem to cheat them all
of death, except

the deafening report of their
collective jaws dropping drowned
the fears in my tears, and

My womb

they wish to had sealed with
royal wax and rolled a stone a-
Cross its mouth
with Centurions stationed both
beside, and yet

they repined everso smug in
their rightwiseness for: what
they set out
to do, they didst so overwell . . .

because it is the cruelest month.

when Thomas

thrust his fingers inside
My Son's nail-

holed hands

they emerged from His palms
not blood-stained
but dotted

with many mustard seeds and

when he withdrew
his hand
from My Son's side

the spear-hole yielded

not more mustard but the un-
cracked kernels

of fresh threshed grain, and

when My Son's tears (shed for
    all
    the world's doubting
    Toms)
were turned to wine and like-

wise washed away all
their fears, I re-

sheathed the sword of Simeon.

Monarchus christus

to think God came
to me
within, a larva in the fullness
of time, mine

and in His time, pupal
was the stage most loved
before the Chrysalis

: Him hung up, dangling even
    as if out to dry

til He burst forth His cocoon!

His soul set free (to show
  us ours might likewise fly), and thus
He fluttered, everso aerie, breath-

less, that is, still as breath (as
    breath withheld, not breath blown

  in) for us, as an ephemera here,
but
for all time He is, the True

genus species: *Monarchus christus*

I too

recently, while in San Diego
making the rounds
of Point Loma Nazarene College (imagine
   that, a college

   and an entire denomination named mostly
   after My Son's
   own hometown) and sitting in on their
Chapel services
looking for reminders of Myself
well, one day

I crossed the line

over the border to Tijuana
during *siesta*
and slipped into a tattoo parlor,
to see about One
for Me

afterall,
My Son, His very Self
had tattoos

and after the time I first
discovered them
there on His sacred but
dead
and oh-so-punct-
uated Body
I decided too, I

should have
a tattoo, at least
One

and so I do

have only One
that now matches My own flowing gown of
Monday morning blue
as always . . . what else; it's a

list, actually . . .
really a series of numbers, in a row
and blue, too
like the little line of the thin vein
it parallels

along My wrist, on the
delicate inside of
My white-as-mother's-milk forearm

where only I
can see

when My sleeve
slips back, slides away a
little
to reveal that

I too
am a Jew

the Speed of Light

all these Flying Crosses
in the sky
put me in the daily mind
of My Son

and His Transfiguration . . .

at thirty-three second intervals (or so
   it seems) day and night, night and
day along the SE/NW flightpath
for Runway 37R and

My home

that at High Noon
receives along with all of *terra firma*
Me and all those other
scarecrows likewise poised, at attention
in the *novena* pose
: ready for
   the cruciform shadow
   gliding o'er us, somewhere
   between Mach 1 and

   the Speed of Light

cast, of course, by the Son above;
it's the Flying Cross

but, seen from on High
when moisture-laden clouds (not quite water
   not quite steam) intercede
the Shadow leaps in Magnitude
upon the clouds (e'en from cloud-to-
   cloud) en-

circled by a miraculous concentric rain-
bow (worthy
   of a Noahal vision) formed around
the Crossed Shadow: it soars, twixt

Heaven and Earth

unless
the cross
is flat, itself upon the ground, wooden,
dull, shadow-
less, life-less, before
the hanger, . . . awaiting the

Passenger

Like an Exclamation Point

from the Beginning He
hath inspired "Do
  not do what hath been said

  but do as I hath done." Therein,

lies the difference.
Whether they be first-born
infants in
Pharoah's land, or Abram's
son at Jehovahjireh, even unto
the Innocents sacri-
ficed for

Our only own begotten Son

He hath shone the Way.
as on that Fri-
day evening twilight sky
silhouetted 'gainst

the fading Son
a pin point of Light exclaimed

: No Greater Love!

but the darkness knoweth
It not yet.

The Branch

(from
      the beginning Alpha
  unto the all-consuming Omega)
shall be
      beautiful and glorious,
the Branch
shall be
      excellent and comely

from a rod out of the stem
of Jesse, and
      righteousness grown up
unto David,

and Its leave-
      ing the garden
of Gethsemane

wherefrom transplanted upon
the Golgotha Hill,
shall make
of It and Its limbs
      a trancept
to silhouette the twilight Friday sky
for all the world to Know
thus saith the Lord

: "I am the Vine"

and I ponder, ever in My heart
why My Son must
still be so

tied to the Tree . . .

when I was with Child, I recall

the cravings
for Bread, and Wine, daily

I longed for the crusty-nut
crunch and
the sweet liquid fire that
satisfied the me
I thought I was, but really was
the He
Who would become . . .

I put it out
of my mind . . .
the need, the crave, in me
to satisfy what I now know

was more than me,
the intrauterine plea awash within—
the amniotic sea's undertow

t'was He
would be the yeast, to leaven
and ferment

His followers, and me

who would require
the sacraments of my desire.

If His were the only Tree

in the Garden
if they must forthwith still
taste of some tree
in search

of knowledge of

good
and evil, then let
them eat of My Son

the Fruit of the tree of Jesse
from whom He depends, ever
for their desire

because

He let Himself be hung there
as if out to dry
so that they
might later partake
of His dehydrated body
and
His unleavened blood
so as to have

the Knowledge

of Whom
it thenceforth hath been said
He is

the Apple of His Father's eye

What if His Father

had Him hung instead
on the Tree

in the Garden of Eden . . .

put Him there in the
Person of
breadfruit and grapes and said

"Taste not of it, lest ye live!"

since Adam and Eve were so
hell-bent to swallow
the Knowledge of Good & Evil, like

when the
latterday adams & eves kneel
at the altar and
stick their tongues out
at the Priest

who says, 'This
is His Body, dipped in the Blood'

: they cross themselves,
   fold their hands upon their breasts
   genuflect and smugly
   seat their soulful selves, where-

in the pew thinking for
certain they know
the difference between Good

& Evil, blithefully indifferent to
the aftertaste of

that first rotten apple from Eve

In the Garden

in the East of Eden one
grew a tree
festooned with Knowledge,
not yet Truth,
in Word, nor deed

although the *pomme du jour*
was sweet,
it was, most likely, red and white

what Good it was
or Evil
most now do know

or think they do

: was He thus
   the Apple of
   Gods' farsighted Omnivision . . .

but what about that other latter tree
imperative, it grew
In the Garden
near Gethsemane (His own
   private Appomattox), the
selfsame one upon
Whom hung, the Word

made flesh, in red and white, dribs
and drabs of
bread, and wine
appliquéd, in such a way
as to encourage tasting, yea, even eating

from this tree too

...ss-up

               √henever
              ·mothers mantle

upon ̣̣̣̣, ̣̣̣houlders, so cross-like. I

shuck it, this Monday-morning blue
gown, as if a second skin

shedding it (in ecdyasy), and
wonder, ponder (as
  always)
in my heart

this once white-as-mother's-
milk skin
that now looks, a little

curdled
round the lids, so I layer on
the lamé (gold leaf, of
  course) atop my crinkled crow's feet,

slip into something slinky,
blood-red
not purple, not royal, nor regal but
lipstick-, fingernail-, 5-alarm-
Fire-Engine RED

step into a pair of
crinoline stiletto heels,
3" tall, black and
shiny, as Judas' patent leather

heart, and last and not the least
I trowel
the mascara on, deep and rich and

thick sky blue, cobalt
glow-in-the-dark, hell-on-earth
azure blaze
sprinkled with
a million sequins, a
constellation o'er each eye,

as when before it came to pass

on some Holy Night
I like, on my back, eye-
ing (through the Midnight Clear)
each twinkle, pondering

still,
calm, bright, silent, so Stellar
the Bethlehem night, at peace,
no longer then their

New Testament Barbie™ let be.

Strawberries

put me in the mind
of My Son

at His Deposition

when we lifted Him
down off of His Cross, after
first extracting

the spikes pinioning His Feet

and Palms, and
we lay His battered Body there
red, reddened, redder where
they'd pummeled Him

to the touch
He yielded sweetened redness

staining hands, clothes, the
very cloths I cleansed His swollen
broken Body with,
. . . as once My fingers lingered
when I used to cleanse His
pink chubby natal Flesh, then. . . .

His Body clotted, like

bruised strawberries coagulating
their darkened deep rosé welts

saving It
to be

turned into communal wine

is that what it's like

when I take communion
feeling the crunch of His Body
ground down
to grit upon My molars, packed

into the crevices
the brown dry unleavened bread

crusty, like the brown bark of
the Tree
he placed between My teeth
to bear down upon
at His not-so-ordinary birth

that splintered not as I ground down,
leaving my throat, parched
in need of soothing by

the slightly bitter communal
fruit of the vine
His unfermented Blood
I taste it, yet

slippery, like my lip's blood
flowing, from between my teeth
clenched, grinding flesh at
His not-so-ordinary death

that bittersweet wine
in My mouth, as it gently
washes free the crusty
ground-down grit

all their sins . . .
. . . is that what it's like

and I can swallow now, so
free and easy by
the birth of His Death

as the Way of believing,
then knowing,

again

the difference between
Good and Evil,
not so as to surely perish
because of, or with

but in spite of . . .
oh which, the Greater Temptation

: to still not see the Truth
  for the Trees

the winedark blood

"My Son,
the Flesh & Blood King."

Why me
(at Communion)
am I
the only one
who combines
the Host & Wine in One

within My cup:

there
nestled in My palm
the limpid pool shimmers
in rhythm
to My heartbeat as
the host (as of old)
absorbs the winedark blood

so that saturated, it
sinks beneath
the Cleansing Flood

and I am me no more;

I sup
and He and I
Are—
One again

the way it used to be.

The other neural communi-
cants
stare at me
in awe and wonder (what

else is new) for
the Mother in Blue

whose Communion evermore
and is
(and was)
and forever always will to be: Flesh

of My Flesh;
Bone
of My bone; Blood of My
blood . . .

of Whom

I am
still well favored

My Mona Lisa lips tell

It all
Or should, how

In the beginning

Pangs, about to be swaddled,
Like death
Attended me while all around
Us knelt
Wonder-full amazements as

I pondered in My heart

If it were some kind of cruel
Knock-knock joke (Who's there / Marry /
    Mary who / Merry Christmas); thus I was
Pronounced at 14—
What did I know, virgin
In more ways than this

Til all, around again me, jeered

The birth of still another new religion
Just what the world needed
While I stood, this time, idly by
In anguished splendor, but in blue as
Always, wondering if

It is finished

And yet
Only Picasso
Ever got it almost right,

When
The Bust of Sylvette literally cracked

A smile

if I lived in Seattle

at Christmastime
I'd have committed suicide

a long time ago

it's bad enough
as it is
each year
over and over and over again
in Bethlehem,
PA
with the steel mills all shut down
and now the K-Marts are too

but I take down
nonetheless
each year at this time
the plaster of paris statuettes
of us,
Myself and all the others
that I made

especially the baby

unwrap him from his swaddling
tissues
to place him in the cardboard crèche

the other figurines I awake
from their
nearly yearlong
hibernation
place the ducks upon the looking glass

arrange the sheep
and cows
in nestled mute array about
the manger

to make the
perfect configuration
in space & time
just so
(will I get it right
  this year . . . ?)

I install
the shepherds, wise men, and
the sundry angels who
remain aloof

while the baby's Ffathers
and I
look on in awe

and wonder
can this be me

it happens to
each year at this time

when
I see the pained reminders

to be put away—
safe
in hibernation
well before Easter

but there's
Hope
with each new birth
that he won't have

to commit

in mea memoria

on a hill faraway
stands, *in mea memoria*, an
old Rugged Cross
decidedly very UpperCase;

X marks the Spot

like latterday Pirates who
abbreviate their *cache en vellum*
with the selfsame Grecian phoneme em-
bracing it likewise for
their about-to-be buried treasure

as on that day
when they, with little x's on
: My Son's palms and feet, upon His brow
   along His side
marking the Spots
to pierce,
so that foreveraftermore and

more real & imagined followers fashion-
ably adorn
with gold and silver reminiscents
: on their ears, at their necks, upon their
   breasts, and
   wrists, even on their lapels

causing me to also reminisce . . .
the day so long ago when Romans played

Pin the Cross on Jesus

some women

wear a locket round their throat
with an inside picture of
their child
or
children,

on a chain

I do too,
sort of;

on my chain though hangs
My firstborn Son,
stretched out
on a
little cross

actually

many other women wear it too (and
   some even
   kiss it) around their necks to
dangle, pendulous

between their breasts

so many so . . . I'm jealous (but
   it is my fate, no, it is
   My blessing
   as the mother of mothers, to

   endure) just
the same
it bothers me to see theirs there,

somewhat likened to My Own

and yet on mine,
only on mine,

I see . . . a baby

an infant, diapered, fresh and clean
but stuck through hands and feet
with pins, bleeding
and crying

crying for His mother

la Madonna del Vita Nuova

sometimes I just have to
console myself

with the fact
that I
once was

la Madonna del Vita Nuova

no, I was
la Madonna Nuovissimo
the star of

stars *stesso bellemissimo* of
heaven above

yes but, that was then . . .
because now
I am
just *Vecchio*

as
the *Festa de Il Redentore*
entices
ospites a turistes
into the *duomo*

for a sheer
glimpse

of
my *stesso fantastica gloriosa*

except that
the way they file by
at this viewing
makes me

on display
feel little more
than

la Madonna del Morte Dolorosa

if there is a universe somewhere

parallel
to this one of ours

a little bit ahead
or some
behind the time of now

I wonder if
God let me have
a baby girl instead, just to see

what difference it might make . . .

I wouldn't have to circumcise, bar
mitzvah Her,
or rear Her so clan-destinely, and

detail where it is
exactly
babies come from, thus

in a world, likened unto ours
parallel, transverse, trap-
ezoidal, or whatever

surely they'd not nail Her to a
tree—but,

if She did it all the same, too

the miracles of water, wine,
and blood;
the fish, the flesh, the bread, the mud;
everything . . .

the giving up, the giving in

some healing, some disappointments—no,
a lot of disappointments . . .

a kiss the Kiss, the some
denying, then the dying, and
the rising; plus,

the final taking-leave—

so, I see, now
there would have to be a Tree

all over again
again,
a little bit ahead

or some behind the times

ever since His birth

I thought My Son looked a little
Crosseyed

but Joseph, of course
passed it off
(maybe because he's a man . . .)
saying, oh, He'll

grow out of it

I tried to dismiss
My feelings, tried not to
ponder in My heart
My maternal apprehensions

but sure enough, as
He grew older
through those lean teen years and well
into a limber young manhood
I could

still just discern, faroff
the slightest Crosseyed flicker
in His vision,
everso, but still just there . . .

sometimes in a faraway gaze
as a lazy azure blur veils, just out
of focus

Joseph, still, dismissed it as
a muscle thing
that would be self-correcting
or He could just see
a Specialist someday, that it wouldn't
never ruin his eye-
sight; I

of course, demurred to the

Penul-
timate Descendant of the 42 Generations

oh, I do remember it all, it
disquiets me yet
as I
recall . . . on a Hill Faraway

how He stumbled forward
fell, onto His knees
as if the Weight of the World were
upon His narrow shoulders
while He

: eyed the Cross

and I
still I ponder in My heart
Father Knows Best

God Is

on my tongue, at
Holy Communion the Host
comes home to roost

in a Way

I had but nought
envisioned; as
if from the first

the Vision of Him in me
were mine, alone

not unlike the melting wafer
transporting Its substance
along my throat, pulsing
through my very veins, to dis-
solve with-

in the core of me, until

His sweet essence
flowed in me, and I

in turn pronounced His name
Lord of All, as He
lay down His sweet head

against my breast
and I kissed the Man-
na from Heaven on His soft baby
face, while He nuzzled me

and I, verily,
the First of all His miracles

was on His tongue

David intoned

first,
the Lord is my Shepherd
and ever since, the

flock hath not wanted, of Him

manifesting Himself as
the ram in the thicket til I

became the fair ewe

and He lay in the manger, like
Mary's little lamb
then 'twas Transfigured in-

to the Lamb of God

by the Great I Am
Who even with ninety and nine
in the fold

hath everknown
the eternal pricelessness of
only
one Lost Sheep

in Green Pastures.

I was told I

was carried by
Enue, Elizabeth's elder sister
a fortnight past my

natal day

into the hallowed hall
to be offered there before
the Lord (a
   sort of earthly redundancy,
   really; no Gabriel present, yet
   nor

   needed. Yet.) toward a High
Priest (him
   as always)
presenting me
holding me, as if he held

the Body of the Lord (no such
   luck, also yet) be-

held Our senses, a-
nointing all five
by thumb, and oil
: ears, eyes, nose, mouth, and
   breast

and on parchment wrote Our name

while the three burnt tufts
of Our hair
smoldering in a nearby brazier
wafted heavenly,
a sweet-smelling sacrifice

in the twilight evening sky

the night before Gabriel

appeared to me
what dreams I dreamed

: I lay at the base of the Tower of Babel

and I heard a
pastiche of
Fiat lux Ecce Homo El Shedai

Getsemani *Got spricht ze jedem nur, eh er*

Ihn macht Sauve qui peut MUERTE

Transfigurazione **Evangelium**
Vitae Faux

Amix Annunciazione **O FOS EN TE SKOTIA**

FAINES Deposizione Dis-moi ce que tu manges,

Et je dirai ce que tu es **Donum**
Vitae Je m'en

vais preparer un endroit por vous *Kommt's uber*

Mich wie Himmelslust! Nativita **Immanuel**

Eucarestia MADONNA DEL
MORTE

DOLOROSA Crocefissi Allegria!
Consummatum est Vive
le Roi!

when I awoke (or so I
  thought) the shadow, not of a Tower, but a
Cross lay across My bed, and

Our Body

if he came to me today

how he did so long ago
unannounced

to pronounce
The impending conception
I would instead
be expected
in this day and age
to scream "RAPE!"

. . . would the painters
then portray

me
for ever after
locked in some dyspassionate
struggle
with my Gabriel-like assailant,
thus:

in full grapple his
knife'd
be at my throat
with my blue sweat-
shirt
hiked up half off of
my head,
my panicking stick-fingers

groping to gouge his eyes (as
  instructed in my
  'Attack-the-Attacker Seminar')

but because the illustrators
are always male
from their perspective

they'd detail
how his celestial knee
deflects my desperate would-be
kick into
his sacred, sanctimonious
crotch

or,
probably they would
picture me
as taking it—
lying down

passive
submissive
even introspective, pondering

in my heart
"Why me, Lord?"

praying, just to
survive
the immaculate violation
so that
early on in the term then, I'd simply
abort Him,

go for counseling, and
get on with
my life
and never after think twice forever

how I would save my son
from the Cross

what a loss

I awakened in a sweat, wet

damp and moist
: fecund from . . . such of a dream?

as I dream, and re-dream

in remembrance of
that time
I could scarcely conceive,
of It, the why
the how, except when I

peruse, re-read, and ponder in my heart
the passage in Isaiah, Six
that nightly re-occurs, a visitation-
vision of the hex-winged seraph whom
before I have so often fallen,

unclean was I, unworthy am I

and yet it flew to me, hovered
bearing the living coal, in tongs
to lay upon my lips

and was purged of me,
any earthly iniquity;
thus was I
made ready, to utter with My lips

"The Word is Now Made Flesh"

apart of a dreamscape, as if
by Dali portrayed
to be
: purified at last, for My Son's

   womb-to-tomb care

Gott spricht zu jedem nur, eh er ihn macht.

Yes, You spoke to me
As You made me

And I felt Your hands upon me, for
I knew Your Spirit was in
The making. And My spirit,
Called out: *"Gib mir Gewand."*

Then was I clothed in flesh.

But later, much later,
Came Your Spirit upon me, to
Me, over Me. In Me.
And You made My Son—Our Son—
Then, I felt Your hands upon Me

All over—All Over, again.

And, again, and forever,
I say,

"Gib mir die Hand."

the Omega Love Child

I loll about My
Monday morning nearly dawning bed a-
skew, a Gustav Klimt figure
study in

My linen blue ethereal negligée

beneath which (barely seen) my flesh
conceals, as under alabaster
the pre-conceived Word: about to be

the Omega Love Child
brought about
without
the Alpha Act.

Around me be-
jeweled pains of
(blood) stained glass
reflect the rosy-fingered Eastern hue in-
suffle sprinkle sparkle tinkle and
a soul-full purl

: my senses of me, thus
  all aroused alert alive

as if I prostrate lay in wait
for It,
and for far more than

just "The Kiss"

thus, duly recorded

—after Psalm 23

in the City of David

led along the right path
for His Word's sake

in a stable prepared for me
in the presence of strangers
I lie down on

pastoral straw while

my head's
anointed with goodness and
surely mercy-
ful sweat drops of blood, and

lo, Jesse
and all the heavenly host
they comfort me for

here the Shepherd is My Lord

as His communal blood runs
over ever
the cup of me with its waters
still, now; forever

in His temple
Me, He shall dwell, all

the days of My Life (is His)
even
though I walk through the
shadow of the Cross

I will fear not.

What
shall I not want?

O Little Heart of Bethlehem

how still you beat in me this night
of deep and dreamless sleep
as dark streets shine
free from the hopes and fears
of those who lie for

He's about to be borne, within me,
as angels keep their watch about us
in this world of sin and
call forth the Dawn of Light, hark

: it heralds the Son of Peace's birth-

right around me strewn the gifts will be
from Hope chests beating
to a different drummer's pulse within
the boy's enlivened hearing, while
the world awaits to rejoice, to receive

His entrance

casts out the dark within, without as
silent stars go by I
prepare my heart, anew, this year to be
the Bethlehem wherein My Lord,
My Son, and I, can thus be born again,

"Come. Come, quickly . . . "

oh, how redundant

those poor poor
shepherds on
My Son's
frightfully frigid
natal night

brought to Him
a gift,

their single
solitary best
begotten present

a newborn lamb, a

living sacrifice
holy, acceptable

while all I
could think of
before offering

my thanks
to their offering

was, oh, that
poor poor

ewe

kneeling at the Manger

staffs at their sides, hushed

mouths agape, reeking not
of frankincense and myrrh, but

of linseed oil, sulfur, pitch, and
tar, these rough men
stare, stunned
by My Son's birth, shocked in

amazed gazing, at Him.

Their faces though I recognize, they're
the providers

of the Paschal lambs, at Passover

for the Temple, they breed and they
take from the ewes their firstborns to
bleed and suffer, sacrificed

to atone for Israel's sin, but

when their shepherd eyes meet mine
I see on their adoring faces a

glimpse of mute surprise, some

wonder; in an eyebrow's rise dis-
belief, while something
in their furtive sidelong glances
causes me to further ponder
more, for

they have been trained
to know a sacrificial lamb when

they see One

at the center of

the manger
I lie, wide-eyed

in pain, in joy, in pain, in
joy, panting the first advent
athwart my isthmus

as the purple candle's lit, white light
serene, in hope, silent bright

in the Holy Night like

the single solitary star, above
it twinkleth, in mine eyes, shining on
the golden straw, about me
while the lowing, bleating filleth the
air, and me; I gasp

at what hath been wrought

for, verily, verily, it hath come to pass
just as 'twere foretold.

Beside me, now, spilled forth
the water and the blood, the tiny
body: alive, to eat, as if manna, sweet

and wise, gifted; I recline, at rest, in

peace,
having awaited Him, as babe, at last
He hath become the

Center of the Known universe.

un der nachtmusick

at . . . The Nightwatch

they say the angels sang
on high
that a heavenly chorus
heralded the way, to

The Way

but I, pondering
in my heart the beat
of a different drummer,
cocked my ear long before
dawn, for

underneath, as if
in contrapuntal strain
I heard in *basso profundo*
what no one else could
or would

: the voice of one
    crying in the wilderness

in our floating baby

days
not all were cherubim
nor seraphim

I oft bespied
a weighty babe aflutter
whose natal face
belied infant John's, dearest
young coz, among

the lofty retinue
while
we at rest our leisure kept

and yet, on guard
a little
whereall they would hover o'er
Our heads, attendeth us

little ones banner clad, aswarm
all pudgy, Reu-
benesque fingers, arms, and toes

lo, the puerile angels flit
to and fro
murmuring aloft of
michelangelo

defying gravity with their looks
of *cupidita*s, not *caritas*
nor e'en *veritas* . . .
but poised in flight, arrows drawn
bows held just back, thus
and so
their darts to planted be

all in the name of Love

which one?
eros? agape? philos?

and one, in
my memory re-appears, wherewith

about his infantine visage is
a hint, cast sharp, against
the Sun, the silhouette of a

betrayer

pink-faced incubus, Judas, like-
ened in infantile disguise
flits about, at arm's length
in the puffclouded cobalt skies (whose

  whispers:
  baseborn, bantling,
  and by-blow
  though

  rarely Love-child
  echo,

  still) as if newly
stepped down from Time's
winged chariot there

hovering ever near

My Son; while with a sigh, I
maternal e'er alert
to that one, lingerer, there

eyes aslant, lips puckered
about to be

pursed

with a haunting J. Iscariot frown
oh, yon one
so profiled in that
Light
hath he about him a

lean and hungry look

by doing good

in the very beginning the
village gossip
she'd profaned My name, before

and at His Virgin Birth and yet

I later aided her
the time she'd stood

outside Our Door
while He, a Son of only 12
looked on

at she who'd
let her hearth fall dark
and so applied to me (when
    none within our town
    would care) for

: Light and heat . . .

I thus replied,
"Take (not just a coal or two
    lest they'd alone lose

    flame) this pot of coals to
    customary carry

    home upon your head"; so
very nearly like the time
My Son replied to . . .

: 'oh Master,
    how ought we

    to treat our enemy?'

April fools

the first at eight, the last at
thirty-three

the best perhaps at twelve

when for three

days, how long else would He—no
when He
first planted His minis-

Tree in the Great
Temple Hall and sat, enthroned (Who not
   wholly filled yet
   their holy chair [His not yet
   throne]) and surrounded
by the aged priestly throng; not the first

not the last, but

the best Paschal April, for
not their profane
knowledge, but properly taught for

prophet-

izing His Messias'
dead rejection, as His Father's Business
Man low-
ly death, whence He practice predicted the
un-
lawfull led
without an ear to hear, who

will not then, there . . .
nor in His twelfth year, here

"no bed of Procrustes"

for He
My Son, at eighteen then

would sleep not on the wood-
planed bed
His father'd shaped (nor

   on any ordinary
   bed of nails not yet custom-
   made for

   The True

   fakir) but rather
didst prefer to sit on it at rest
all
the night long
covered barely by the One thin
blanket He
acknowledged and

lay down His sweet Head

upon the One and only homespun
wool
-en pillow I'd ever

hand-made for the Lord,

deigning even then a king-sized
bed, disdained instead
on earth, He said, til He reclined

at length upon the only couch
fit truly for a King,
where X mark'd the spot

   : at the crotch of a cross

at the marriage

in Cana
why were they so surprised

He changed the water
into wine
afterall He had

done it all before, ceasing then

to surprise me evermore
(in particular
  after that clear dark cold night
  as
  the Spirit He Himself

  It seized upon me) when He
changed my water (that
  was the first)
into blood and then into
eventual immortal and not the least
communal
wine (and that
  was not the last)

and back, again

and forth
unto the Marriage Supper of the Lamb
and thence

into the Springs of Living Water

welling up with just so much practice
until made
Perfect

when He, the Groom (this time)
comes back, again to
catch up His Bride in the wide bright sky

and tears
shall be no more
for not will this mother weep anon

at that
her Son's at last

Rite

When My Son

raised Lazarus from the dead

he never forgave Him
oh, . . . his sisters
loved Him even more than before

but Lazarus never got over
being
called forth from His Father's
presence, since

: a sparkle in the eye, the warmth of
  a hug, a tug on the heart, hearing
  his name—'Laz-a-rus?'—
  whispered There aloud would

never be . . . the same again here; oh
yes, I know the feeling, for

His Father breathed in me,
once
and I've
never been the same

nor has the world, and

although My Son lived (and
   died) to forgive him,
and loved
his sisters in return

I now know . . . of all the miracles
My Son performed
that's the one I'm everso glad

He never did again, on earth . . .

"Jesus wept,"

so they say,

thus,
purporting Him to be
the Ultimate Soul of Brevity.

And yet
it was just part of a Flood-
plan
so that, according to hearsay

and I know
His Other Father shed far more
than just a tear,

For I was there.

And there have been
before and since
such Lamentations
and wailing and gnashing
of teeth

ashes and sackcloth,
salty lashes, and
runny noses, heads of hair
to dry
His tear-stained dusty feet;

and yet I
only I
as Mother of mothers,
I'm the paradigm of lachrymose
grief,
ever pondering in my heart

why my water broke
and what those myriad tears
of His

have since then washed away . . .

accused of adultery

the woman brought before My Son
accused of adultery

was me

. . . could have been me, they ringed
with their stony eyes and
hardened hearts
fingers itching, bodies aching
to be next, too late to be the first

to cast a stone before the One
Who would know
what it's like

to bear the Last Straw (Light

  as a Cross) if Joseph
hadn't stepped forward,

which is what
My Son
probably wrote in the sand, in
Belshazzar font, those oh so many
years ago

: Where is the man?

At the Wedding

of Jairus' daughter to
Mary and Martha's brother
My Son
breathed new Life into the vow

: til death do us part

for they two were more than mere
ornaments atop a cake; they
were one of the rings
for the circus at-
mosphere there where

the leper and the parlytic
seated the guests, the
lame pranced the
"Hava Negila," the blind carried
Lazarus around on the chair, and
the lad with the barley

loaves & fishes showed all (but
    the foolish virgins) The Way
to the banquet table to

await the Marriage Supper
of the Lamb,
food for thought enough

for the Afterlife after their death.

Also at the Wedding

where the children chanted

: Jairus' daughter
Martha's brother
sittin' neath the Tree
k-i-s-s-i-n-g

I pondered are they the new
Adam & Eve who
brought all this to pass . . .

: Father, Father, up above
help me kiss the one I love

and was he answered, thus

: sinner, sinner, down below
pucker up and let her go!

Peradventure, there begat
the line of Adam's
race that brought My Son
into His Garden, for
the Apple still

never far falls from the Tree

the New Golden Rule

when doing unto others
became passé, for
only what they'd done unto them

My Son (in His

   customary re-write-the-Laws
   role) assayed His followers
to be (in His us-
   ual parabolic Way) likened unto another Mary who

did unto Him
with the broken jar of
spike-
nard, with her tears,
and with her hair upon
His not quite yet

nail-scarred feet,
where she there shewed forth

the New True Love Commandment

: to do unto others as
  you would do

  unto Him

of the Parable of

the fowls of the air

lost
to the Pauline, Petrine, Lucan,
and
Johanine traditions (*et al.*)

but found

on the road to Emmaus, He said

on, lo, some dark drear cold
night
hardscrabbling in the bluster
of the snow blown wind and gale

In The Bleak Midwinter, they

flitted, forth hither and yon
for warmth, for food, for shelter
from the storm
until some Adamic Son
bewailed
their feathered plight and invited

them in-

to his house, of many mansions, in

nouveau Assisi style; and yet
they would not, no
matter howso'er much he enticed
their flight
through speech nor signs nor
mighty wonders, deeds, or words
until,
he thought (within a Word,
  why) I'll

. . . become a bird

My Son
thus spake,

at His Last Supper

He re-wrote the Book
actually, The User's Manual
for the Epicureans
when He broke His

Body, and dipped It into

the Chalice wherein
careful not, to spill a drop of
His sweet blood, said

: Eat, Drink, & Be Merry
  for tomorrow I die

and ever since we
have been
The New Epicureans
when we sup now and
forever
at His Banquet Table

: Eating, Drinking, & Making
  Merry, all

because He died

so that you and I might
live our tomorrows forever
and ever and ever . . .

and ever . . .

the night that Peter slept

the night before My Son sweat
great drops of blood
he dreamed in fits full of

the scritch-scratch
needleprick of thorns through scalp

grating 'gainst skull and

nails pounded, ripping flesh,
cracking, piercing bones

and myriad fiendish splinters
snagged and hooked
prickly flesh, each follicle
along the striped back (especially
  His bruised welts) along

his buttocks, even
his calves, and
sagging arms each hair a tracer
for the wooden barbs
that cling and claw
while (as at His own

  private Appomattox) the spittle

dripped (not
  His own) hung
off his nose and lips, but gobbed
his beard while

a fickle *vox populi* jeered his
death-mask nakedness

but
Peter awoke
with a

start at My Son's pained rebuke . . .

yet so breathed in relief to know
'twas only a dream; nonetheless, it

did come True.

Regulis Pacis

they call Him
Lamb of God, Lion of the
Tribe of Judah, but I

call Him
the Frog of God; and my

favorite metaphor
of Him is the Little Tadpole,
but before that

He was just so much quivering jelly
from an egg laid
by some shimmering ectoplasm Who

transmogrified Himself
through The developmental

stages Of

to become the Frog of Man, yea
even a Treefrog
the very rarest of True genus species
: a *Hylum christus*,

who was transcended
with a Kiss
into

the Prince of Peace

Acknowledgements

the following poems have been published or will be published in the following places:

"an immaculate conception" in *The International Poetry Review*
"**Agni Dei**" in *The Christian Century*
"**Theotokos**" in *Christianity & the Arts*
"on Good Friday afternoon" in *Christianity & the Arts*
"**Amor omnia vincit**" in *ProCreation*
"after His death" in *Pacific Coast Journal*
"**Monarchus christus**" in *Christianity & the Arts*
"I too" in *Art Centering*
"the Speed of Light" in *The Penwood Review*
"The Branch" in *First Things*
"when I was with Child, I recall" in *The Prairie Star*
"If His were the only Tree" in *First Things*
"In the Garden" in *Cornerstone*
"I am playing dress-up" in *The Ravens Perch*
"Strawberries" in *The Christian Courier*
"is that what it's like" in *George & Mertie's Place*
"the winedark blood" in *Books & Culture*
"My Mona Lisa lips tell" in *The Rolling Coulter*
"if I lived in Seattle" in *First Things*
"**in mea memoria**" in *Driftwood 2003*
"some women" in *Art Centering*
"**la Madonna del Vita Nuova**" in *Tule Review*
"if there is a universe somewhere" in *ProCreation*
"ever since His birth" in *ProCreation*
"God Is" in *Christianity & the Arts*
"David intoned" in *Poetry Motel*
"if he came to me today" in *Second Glance*
"I awakened in a sweat, wet" in *Driftwood 2003*
"oh, how redundant" in *The Christian Century*
"kneeling at the Manger" in *The Christian Century*
"**un der nachtmusick**" in *Advent 2000*
"'no bed of Procrustes'" in *Driftwood 2004*
"at the marriage" in *The Penwood Review*
"'Jesus wept,'" in *George & Mertie's Place*

"accused of adultery" in *First Things*
"At the Wedding" in *Mars Hill Review*
"Regulis Pacis" in *Wavelengths*

"Accused of Adultery" appeared in *Grace Notes*, an anthology of the 'Best of the Best' poems published in *First Things*, edited by Joseph Bottum and Dana Gioia.

"Agni Dei" and "kneeling at the Manger" will appear in *Taking Root in the Heart: 31 Poets from the Christian Century*, an anthology of the "Best of the Best," edited by Jill Pelaez-Baumgartner.

Seventeen of the poems in this manuscript first appeared in *Mary Speaks of Her Son*, published in 2008 by Finishing Line Press.

"Theotokos" was set to music in a contrapuntal arrangement with the *"Stabat Mater"* prayer to form "'*Stabat Mater*' with 'Theotokos" for orchestra and chorus; words, by Jacopne da Todi/Innocent III and Carl Winderl; music by composer Rick Arnest, on March 16, 2017.

Another five poems, from *Mary Speaks of Her Son* (*"Theotokos,"* *"Monarchus christus,"* "The Branch," *"un der nachtmusick,"* and *"Regulis Pacis"*) were set to music for piano and soprano by Composer Victor Labenske and premiered, March 2nd, 2017. Audio recordings of these pieces can be accessed by visiting: https://www.youtube.com/results?search_query=victor+labenske+mary+speaks+of+her+son

Gratitude

Thanks eversomuch to:
Leah Heute de Maines
Christen Kincaid
Elizabeth Maines McCleavy
Kevin Maines
and the entire FLP Team

I am blessed, by all of their efforts on behalf of my poetry and me.

Author Bio

Christened in the Polish National Trinity Catholic Church and baptized in the Church of the Nazarene, **Carl Winderl** is the beneficiary of his grandmothers alternately ferrying him one Sunday to a Catholic Mass and the next to a Protestant worship service. *The Gospel According . . . to Mary* is a reflection of those combined influences over the years.

He earned a Ph.D. in Creative Writing from New York University and an M.A. in American Literature & Creative Writing from the University of Chicago.

Formerly, he was a Professor of Writing in the LIT/JRNLSM/WRIT/LANG Dept., at Point Loma Nazarene University, in San Diego. After he left PLNU he lived for two years in Zagreb, Croatia, where he served as a missionary educator for the Church of the Nazarene; currently he lives in Kyiv, Ukraine, where he serves in a similar assignment.

Finishing Line Press has published three other collections of His Marian poetry: *Mary Speaks of Her Son* (2005), *la Via de La Croce* (2008), and *Behold the Lamb* (2015).

In addition, his Marian poetry has been linked with Thomas Merton, Pier Paolo Pasolini, John Donne, *et al.*, at—https://udayton.edu/imri/mary/p/poems-by-carl-winderl.php—under the auspices of the International Marian Research Center & Library, hosted by the University of Dayton, where his Rosary sequence of twenty poems can be found under the title of *Les Mysteres*.

Additional Praise for *The Gospel According . . . to Mary*

No one can take a familiar phrase, word, or story and make you experience it differently than Carl Winderl. With his references to biology, mathematics, literature, tattoos, holocaust, grief and love, Winderl helps us see something we thought we already knew—only now we know it better. Reading *The Gospel According . . . to Mary* had me asking, "How did he do that?" Sometimes I was talking about God showing his love for all of creation. Sometimes I was talking about Carl showing his love for language.

> —**Dean Nelson**, author of *God Hides in Plain Sight: How to See the Sacred in a Chaotic World*; director, Journalism Program, Point Loma Nazarene University; director, "Writer's Symposium By The Sea"

The voices that have reverberated down through the ages, since those momentous times—Christ's conception, martyrdom, and resurrection—have been primarily male. The main female interlocutor is the Virgin Mary and yet her voice is recorded in only four passages of the Bible. Thus it remains to the poets to articulate the visions, hopes, and sorrows of the Blessed Mary, which Carl Winderl does with joy, verve, insight, and even playfulness. This brilliant collection of poems pulses with Carl's deep-seated faith and his abiding love for the Virgin Mary. It is such a welcome gift to this sore world.

> —**Marcia Whitney-Scheneck**, the former publisher of *Christianity and the Arts*, is the author of *Triptych*, a historical, literary novel on a Medieval Black Madonna (Amazon)

Carl Winderl, a Protestant poet with Catholic sensibilities writing in the voice of Mary, graphically and poignantly plumbs the depths of one of the greatest mysteries of all time—not just that God deigned to become Incarnate in human flesh, but that the sovereign God of the universe intimately shared His mission of redemption with a simple peasant girl. Winderl's terse, often startling, and breath-taking Marian insights are a revelation to behold.

> —**Dr. Kent R. Hill**, Senior Fellow and co-founder of the Religious Freedom Institute, Russian historian, author of *The Soviet Union on the Brink*; former president of Eastern Nazarene College; Assistant Administrator of the U.S. Agency for International Development; and Senior Vice President of World Vision. Hill came into full communion with the Catholic Church in 2013.

Additional Praise for *The Gospel According . . . to Mary*

This narrative collection invites the reader to grapple with the intersection of Mary's Biblical image and her lived experience as the author imagines it. *The Gospel According . . . to Mary* is an abstract exploration of the personal crisis of Christ's death, lost to time. Winderl interrogates the mystery of Mary's human experience, discovering her heart through both the malleable lens of history and the unchanging chorus of the natural world. Bold and subversive, sacred and pure, *The Gospel According . . . to Mary* is worth the grapple.

> —**Deborah Joy Corey**, author of *Losing Eddie*, *The Skating Pond*, and *Settling Twice: The Essays*

Winderl strikes again. In his newest collection of poetry, he once again manages to bridge the gap between Catholic and Protestant beliefs about the Mother of Christ. Mary, the one voice to travel the path of Christ, from birth to death, finds life in Winderl's words. Neither deified, nor merely human, Mary speaks from experience as she lends voice to the path Jesus wandered from joyous birth to agonizing death. Each poem in the collection masterfully captures a scene in the life of Christ and lends human emotion to flesh out the story. With power and poise, the words leap from the page and imprint a flesh and blood woman into the minds of the readers. Her voice resonates with our own experiences and forges a connection with one of the most mysterious figures in the Bible. Prepare to be swept up in the story and left with a new perspective on a life so often tucked into the background.

> —**Zachary Winderl**, author of *Atom & Go: Genesis* and its forthcoming sequel *Atom & Go: Trinity*; also, he's the son of Carl Winderl

Carl Winderl portrays the Virgin Mary eternally "pondering in her heart" specific moments of the life of Christ from her Motherly perspective, organically brought together as a whole, like a multisided jewel refracting light differently each way we turn it. The poems invite us to not only observe, but prayerfully participate in her sorrow, wonder, and joy—and this joy is her Gospel, sometimes quiet, sometimes triumphant, transfiguring poetry into songs of praise.

> —**Josh Seligman**, editor of *Foreshadow* and Graduate of Earlham School of Religion's Ministry of Writing Program and Point Loma Nazarene University's Writing/Journalism Program

Additional Praise for *The Gospel According . . . to Mary*

These poems shouldn't work for me. First, I'm not really a poetry guy. Limericks, sure. But apparently those don't count. Second, a Boomer Protestant white man writing in the voice of an ancient Catholic icon? Who happened to be a middle eastern mother? It just doesn't add up. Luckily, I'm not a math guy either. This collection jolts me awake. These poems alternately fill my heart with beauty, then punch me in the gut. They infuse scripture with fresh imagination, fresh perspective, fresh empathy. They take me deeper. They draw me to consider Mary's unique place in creation, while also identifying with her. These poems help me to feel something new about Jesus, while invoking chemistry, the holocaust, diamonds, and tattoos. They're best taken in slowly and a sip at a time, like good bourbon. These poems work so well for me.

> —**Craig Dockery**, Musician & Creative Director, but in a midwestern kind of way; most recent album, "Hymns for Trucks"

Always moving, always thoughtful, always profound, Mr. Winderl's poems should be read with great care and great openness. I hope and trust Mother Mary still ponders these things in her heart.

> —**Robert Benson**, Writer of *Between the Dreaming and the Coming True* and *Dancing on the Head of a Pen*

CPSIA information can be obtained
at www.ICGtesting.com
Printed in the USA
FSHW010353200221
78783FS